Hotel Me

Other books by Ron Overton

Dead Reckoning (Street Press)
Love on the Alexander Hamilton (Hanging Loose Press)

Hotel Me
Poems for Gil Evans and Others

by
Ron Overton

Hanging Loose Press
Brooklyn, New York

Copyright © 1994 by Ron Overton

Published by Hanging Loose Press, 231 Wyckoff Street, Brooklyn, New York 11217. All rights reserved. No part of this book may be reproduced without the publisher's written permission, except for brief quotations in reviews.

Printed in the United States of America
10 9 8 7 6 5 4 3 2 1

Hanging Loose Press gratefully acknowledges a grant from the Literature Program of the New York State Council on the Arts. The author wishes to thank the New York Foundation for the Arts for a writing fellowship which helped in the completion of this book.

Some of these poems first appeared in the following publications: *Bluefish, Brook Spring, Commonweal, Hanging Loose, The Journal of All Thought, Long Island Quarterly, Open Places, Massachusetts Review, Street Press, Spacecorn, Styrofoam, Transfer* and *Williwaw*.

Cover art by Ellen Nora

Library of Congress Cataloging-in-Publication Data

Overton, Ron.
    Hotel Me : poems for Gil Evans and others / Ron Overton.
       p. cm.
    ISBN 1-882413-09-1 (cloth) : — ISBN 1-882413-08-3 (pbk.)
    1. Evans, Gil, 1912-1988 —Poetry 2. Gil Evans Orchestra
Poetry. 3. Jazz musicians—Poetry. I. Title.
PS3565.V436H67   1994
811'.54—dc20   93-47147
                                                      CIP

 Produced at The Print Center., Inc., 225 Varick St., New York, NY 10014, a non-profit facility for literary and arts-related publications. (212) 206-8465

Contents

1.

Anita's Dance   13
Narrative   14
Bud and Bird   15
The Altoist   17
Hotel Me   18
Real Musicians   19
Catalogue   20
Let's Get Lost   21
Little Wing   22
Record   23
Barracuda   25
I Want You   26
Zee Zee   27
I Dream of Billie Holiday   28
La Nevada   29
Catching the Trane   30
Miles Ahead (Miles Apart)   31
After Mingus   32
Goodbye Pork Pie Hat   33
O. C.   34
Assignment: Who Was George Antheil, and Where?   36
Paris Blues   38
Minimal Suite   39
Variations for Winds, Strings and Keyboards   42
Recital   43
That's Right   44
Beyond Words   45
Teen Town   46

2.

The Branch Will Not Break, But the Jay Might   49
The Economics of Small Losses   50
Midnight   51
Home Movies   52
Match Point   53
Larkin   54

The Acting Program Director Holds a Press
Conference to Explain the Death of the
Challenger Shuttle and Seven Aboard in a
Fiery Cloud of Snow   55
Cold Harbor   56
Poets in Their Youth   57
Blues   58
A.M.   59
Last Rites   60
Four Poems About Distance, in Memory of My Father   61
Untitled   64
Lately   65
Song   66
CVA   67
On the Death of Parents   70
Someone Stopped In   71

3.
Blues in "C"   74

Some of the poems in Part 1 (and Part 3, "Blues in 'C' ") are based on the titles of songs associated with Gil Evans—both his own compositions and his "recompositions" of music by others. The titles were starting points for the writer, but familiarity with individual songs is not essential for the reader. They were simply a way of getting the writing done, as well as a way to acknowledge the special importance Evans' work has held for me, particularly during times of loss and absence.

Thanks to John Clark, who explained that the "hotel" in *Hotel Me* was verb, not noun: touring and tired, you plead "hotel me."

Thanks to Anita and Miles Evans, who have kept the music going.

—R.O.

In memory of my parents

Hotel Me

Anita's Dance

O to be a musician
in Gil Evans'
Monday Night Orchestra
to sing
on a shiny saxophone
any way I want
and then to yell
at the other guys
encouraging their abandon
then drunk
on ardor
we go
off the scale
together
out of sight
to settle
finally
separately
in a rabble of notes
falling
        like snow
vanishing
        like snow

Narrative

Once long ago I used to
win records listen to the radio
and get the questions right
long ago when I knew the answers
and even chat coolly with
the disc jockeys who in jazz
even over the phone talk real slow
and deep never getting excited
the record I remember most was
the record I wanted most you know
that kind of centering of the day
around the mail I was excited and
when it finally came the mailman
thinking calendar or not thinking
or thinking malice folded it
into a large U so it conformed perfectly
to the shape of the mailbox I was
disappointed and sorely mad went
to the post office fast in the Volvo
and the next day he glared at us and
later would put foreign objects
in our mailbox but what was amazing was
after a week between other records
under that steady peer pressure it
flattened out and still is
they say some objects have a good
memory can recall and recover
their first and true selves the point is
I'd like to have that
slow but sure resiliency
that cool plasticity that
always finds home
that jazz

Bud and Bird

for Chris Hunter

bop was for the immortal young
who made a religion of velocity
a cult of nerves
who dreamed of dying young
thus living forever

and they did
and they didn't

the wild calculus of Bird
scaling the wall of strung-out neon night
who rode a vortex of lights
snapping in the synapse

and Bud in exile
estranged to nowhere
who sped too fast across the icy keys
and slipped and fell

Bud and Bird   on the move

and mysterious Monk
who survived   in his hat
tiptoeing across the space between the notes
(Monk busted   someone told me
in the South
and they lifted him from the car
and for three weird days he held
the driver position in his cell
nothing moving but
the riffs inside his head)

Fats dead at 26
Clifford Brown at 25
as though it were a competition
a death jam   a cutting session
some dead in cars
at the end of the road of one-night stands
some gone into their bodies and lost
some swept away by tides of madness

some blinded by the light
some swallowed by the dark
the holy breath sucked out by the dark
inside the horn

someone would shout go go go
and they would go

Bud and Bird   on the move
as though to stop
would mean
an easy target

The Altoist

practicing in the
basement starts low
it could be almost
anybody then
begins
to limber up
others on the band
stand gathering play
a few notes make
adjustments
to their instruments
but somebody's serious
in the basement
he's climbing the ladder
of difficulty
now
it couldn't be
anybody it's Chris
swirls of quick-
silver sound
spiraling off
the top of
the horn until
he comes up smiling
& smiles & laughs
& plays all night
like it's a gift

Hotel Me

if Hotel Me
on that
is really Jelly Roll
and I buy this
to hear the real
Hotel Me
and it sounds
exactly
like Jelly
Roll too then
is there
a Hotel Me
or is it just
a phantom
riff Gil's
little joke
a name for
nothing

        O
just dig the
rollicking
sweet
barrelhouse
stagger of
whatever it is
or
as Phil Woods
once said to
the many occupants
of me
      I don't
keep track
man
      I just play

Real Musicians

for Carla Bley

I'm looking at the group picture
from the European Tour album
and nobody seems to know what to do
everybody's joking around but
nobody looks comfortable Roswell Rudd
has even regressed so far it's
the old class clown chestnut he's
crossing his eyes down the axis
of his cigarette but later

I listen to him play "A New Hymn"
and he seems to know exactly what to do
so comfortable he's not even there
there's just the music
pouring out of him
it's as though this is the one thing
worth doing
and everything else
is just standing around

Catalogue

Sirs:

thank you for
once and for all
clearing up
my abiding confusion
of David 'Fathead' Newman
with Eddie 'Cleanhead' Vinson
but if I may ask
where does Eddie 'Lockjaw' Davis
fit in all of this

Let's Get Lost

listening to Chet Baker
in the dark
listening to Chet Baker
all night in the dark
the last songs
from the movie soundtrack where
"blame it on my youth" becomes
"blame it on my use" (with-
out a hint of irony) and
other syllables simply get lost
in the haze or
are just too hard to say
though the singing
is the pure uncut singing
of a fallen angel
who used us all
and then sang so sweetly
we forgave
an old man who was meant
to die young
it's about staying on too long
about being found when
you want to get lost
listening to Chet Baker
in the dark
the sidewalk rushing up
listening to Chet Baker
all night in the dark

Little Wing

outside it sounds like a train
something is cheeping
in all this gray
and wind

outside it sounds like a rushing river
something is lost
or out of place
something small

Record

1.
Everyone has gone away.
I'm listening to the agile
post-bop saxophone of
Eric Dolphy swoop and dart
in the silence they've left behind.
It's the first day of August, 1984.
He has been dead for twenty years.

2.
The record is called **Last Date.**
It's a live recording, a club in Holland,
genius gliding above local talent....
You can hear the ice cubes click in the glasses
of June 2, 1964, in a club in Holland,
and they did not know this would be the last date,
and they did not know these moments would happen
again and again because of vinyl:

> *re*, of course, meaning *again* or *back*
> *cord*, from *corde*, meaning *heart* or *mind*
> i.e., to bring back to mind, to remember,
> to know something by heart

My arithmetic says he has two months to live.

3.
Some in the crowd are probably dead now too.
Some things are mathematical and clear,
but most things are only probable, a matter of odds,
even such apparent certainties as that we won't
wake up tomorrow and find ourselves still entangled
in the fourth grade, or that the apple will fall,
rather than rise in the August heavens,
because it always has....

And some things aren't clear at all.
I hear a voice suddenly cry out but
can't tell for sure if it's someone outside
in the street now or
someone twenty years ago,
a voice arriving like the light of a star,
urging him on.

4.
Eric Dolphy.
Died: June 29, 1964.
Probable cause of death: heart attack, brought on
          by various complications.
His notes swoop and dart mysteriously,
    dolphin-like, in the air—
        lyrical facts,
            various complications,
                mathematical and clear.

Barracuda

she said while the cat's away
the mouse can play   wanna play
she said I'm listening to Barracuda
do you know that
she said I like the sound of your voice
you sound like a disc jockey
she said how about if I bring
some wine over in my Barracuda
where do you live
where do you live
I'd worked one summer in Bermuda
there was a barracuda around by the boathouse
it had dangerous teeth
she said what do you say champ
wanna take a chance
it had dangerous teeth
small but abundant and sharp
I could hear Barracuda in the background
it was popular that year
not Gil's but another
I could hear it in the background
with its dangerous teeth

I Want You

He's outside the Rialto.
It's 95°, mid-afternoon, but what's playing inside
is a moody melodrama meant for the disappointments
of night. *We can't go on like this. Where is
the happiness we once knew? I want you
more than anything in the world.* All the worn phrases
we say but don't believe when we hear ourselves
in the movies. The music swirls in a soupy
imitation of passion. The voices of course are distant,
tiny, like those of children across a lake.
He smiles at the clichés, knowing they're true,
knowing they're unutterable.
Desire must have its irony, its tongue-in-cheek,
to better silence.

He stays, held there, but won't go in.

Zee Zee

someone
is asleep
in the glow
of the roadhouse

I Dream of Billie Holiday

in my freshman composition course

    she has seen "many things"
    she has "been hurt"

try to be more specific I whisper

      there are run-ons

        you can't tell where one sentence
          ends & another begins

you're tellin' me she replies
    & starts to sing the details

don't explain I say
          holding up my hand

    but she's gone

La Nevada

O motel insomnia

she paraded around
all night in
her lacy underwear

leggy blonde

O sunbelt nights

hour of rogue semis
diesel drunk
crazy for the open road

O liquored dreams
wakeful dreams
heady perfume
black lace

headlights
ghost the wall

O leggy motel
blonde insomnia

Catching the Trane

I only heard Coltrane once, live.

It was Pep's, in Philly, around 1965.

It was when he was being criticized for
    "practicing in public,"

playing long, serpentine solos that would
    last an entire set.

It was hard to hear him—Elvin Jones a din
    of drums in the poor miking,

Jimmy Garrison's bass lines buried under
    the mad hammering of McCoy Tyner....

Trane seemed preoccupied and less than legendary,
    which I suppose he was then,

being well-alive and subject to criticism.
    We left after a set.

I would have stayed longer had I known
    about dying young.

I'm sure he would have too.

Miles Ahead (Miles Apart)

for Dave Bargeron

It's perfectly natural,
the wariness pros feel for
critics and pundits.

The Gold Glove shortstop hides
in the manager's office so
as not to discuss the zen koan

of whether the error
leading to the double play
makes him the hero

or the goat.
He's just doing
the work to be done.

Or, as Gil Evans said
after boisterous praise: *Man,
I just want to play the piano*

and have a band.

After Mingus

we go to Macy's &
in the dead light of fluorescence

& dusk we
snap at each other.

The manikins smile.
They have spread their picnic cloth.

You gliding downward to Perfumes
like Eurydice,

me lost in a crowd
of coats, faces

drowning in glass.
That soft tolling,

no song
to call us back.

for George Adams, saxophonist of the limbic system

Goodbye Pork Pie Hat

played
so slow

and soulful

as though
you knew

this was
the last gig

triple blues

for Prez
for Mingus

gone now too

and too soon
after:

you

O. C.

1.

In 1959
there was talk of this cat
who played a white plastic saxophone

in 1959
you would have to explain you
didn't actually mean a cat

I could see the white plastic saxophone
I could hear it in my mind
it sounded like the ones in woolworths
my father told me not to touch
it sounded stingy and bright

2.

In 1972
I finally saw him in person and
by then he had become acceptable but
by then he had taken up
the violin

it was an afternoon concert
he paced around the stage getting tangled
in the microphone cord
every now and then
dropping his bow into the first couple of seats

enthusiastic fans would return it to him
but he seemed puzzled it had come back

he must have taken too many antihistamines
someone said but I think it was just hard

playing with the sun in your eyes

3.

Anyway it didn't matter
coming up next was the new york bass choir
thirteen basses all going at once

o boy we thought o man

slam stewart would go crazy
humming along thirteen different ways

you couldn't tell if this was way out
or way in

ornette watching from the wings
grinning like a cat
as the sun began to go

Assignment: Who Was George Antheil, and Where?

George Antheil (pronounced än' til), the notorious
"Bad Boy of Music," was a composer who went
   backwards,
or maybe not. He started by upsetting everyone

with his "Airplane Sonata" in 1923, which caused rioting
in Paris, which to me sounds pretty much *de rigueur*
for Paris in 1923, whoever heard of the premiere

of a work in Paris in 1923 where the audience left quietly,
politely comparing impressions and asking about the
   family?
This was followed by his most famous work, *Ballet
   Mécanique,*

featuring pianos, xylophones, percussion, electric bells
and an airplane propeller. In 1927 at its Carnegie Hall
   debut
the audience "booed, whistled, clapped and even hissed."

The "Bad Boy of Music" had struck again! But gradually
   his work,
as will happen if you stick around long enough, was
   accepted.
By 1954 the piece that had shocked Paris and frightened
   New York

was found to be "ebullient and lively...actually pretty
in places." And George "Bad Boy" Antheil begins to
   change.
His work becomes more "dramatic." *(New York Times)* He
   sees that

"a return to the romantic and heroic is natural." *(Time)*
He begins writing "crackerjack scores" for the movies.
   (Time)
I suppose they sensed reform, maturity, the prodigal son's
   return,

and were happy as only the guardians of art can be happy.
And at first you think: Ah yes, middle age. But there are
aberrations in the pattern, little things at first.

In an aside we learn that he re-reads the novels of Stendhal
every year. OK. But he starts writing articles on
 endocrinology
(Hey, isn't that about glands?) for *Esquire*. And finally

this, which should make us stop: "He and Hedy Lamarr
invented a radio-directed torpedo on which they hold
a United States patent." Now we are somewhere else,

now the "Bad Boy of Music," along with the banker's
 daughter
who gave cinematic nudity the go-ahead, has taken the
 propeller
out of the music and hidden it under the sea, where no one

can hear it—his greatest coup, his grandest prank!
"An intense, bright-eyed man," croons *The New Yorker*.
And we think we begin to understand.

Paris Blues

the Yamaha chimes
a shimmery sorrow
too articulate
to last for long

now underneath now
insinuating it-
self around the spare
and sinewy

speech of Steve Lacy's
exile soprano now
content to just comp
along for a

while until O hell
let's start singing (I told
you so) we'll just nod
our heads a lit-

tle from time to time
like wised-up homesick kids
keep in mind it's still
it's still the blues

Minimal Suite

1

Hold your two pointer fingers
about an inch apart
and look off into the distance,
my son says,
and you will see
a sausage.

It's true.

That's very interesting, I say.
Is it really there? he asks.

2

When he leaves,
I try it again.

It works every time.

After a while
I name it:
My Magritte Finger.

3

I lock myself in the john.
It works every time.
A stubby island of flesh.
A sausage.

4

I listen to Thelonious Monk
on my Walkman
all through the night.

The music neither obscures
nor clarifies the matter.

5

Gradually, the excitement of discovery
is replaced by a hazy calm,
an assurance made possible only

by living continuously in the presence
of a predictable, repeatable event.

6

Friends stop trying to call.
My family adjusts to my absence.
He's in the john working on an epistemological problem,
my wife tells insurance salesmen,
who misunderstand, thinking the sarcasm
is directed at them.

7

I sneak out at night
and buy batteries.

8

My family moves away.
There's the smell of fresh paint.
In the silent spaces of Monk's "Bemsha Swing"
I hear the voices of strangers.

9

There are rumors
of a woman President,
of the repeal
of the infield fly rule.

I cannot, in the night,
tell my eyes from the dark.

10

I switch to John Cage,
Sultan of Silence.

11

I believe
the house is empty now.
There is just this:
the quiet transport of blood,
the floating flesh.

12
It is really there
It is real
It is
It

Variations for Winds, Strings and Keyboards
after Steve Reich

parallelograms of gray cement
the eye wants to make rectangular
repeated but slightly different
just as these wisps of cloud are the same
but each slightly different behind
the corner of modern sky-
scraper made of gray parallelograms

wisps of cloud moved by winds
of the blue sky behind them (well
we imagine them to be moving but
so gradually that they inhabit
some space between a photograph
of blue sky and clouds and
blue sky and clouds)

it must be by looking long enough
that they begin to change they
slowly take up their apparent moving
behind the gray slabs of not sky
which stand rock still and
in standing still allow the motion
provide the measure

wisps of cloud moved by winds
repeated but slightly different
parallelograms of gray cement
in standing still allow the motion
of blue sky and clouds (well
we imagine them to be moving but
it must be by looking long enough)

it must be by looking long enough

Recital

your sister
turning the pages for
you then

you return the favor
turning the pages
for her

now that seems fair
I thought
and sisterly

then she again
turns the pages for
you making

a fine music
a harmony of sisters
of your fair hair

suddenly brown
against the raven black
of her long hair

That's Right

Miles is dead.

So what.

There's plenty
to go around.

Rumor at the record store
is fact on the news.

(They get it wrong
of course.)

So what.

Miles is dead.

That's right.

Like all his notes,
perfect timing…

Montreux
the perfect resolve.

Miles is dead.

That's right.

That's right.

Beyond Words
   for Mark Egan

Yes
there are some things
that elude words &
simply must be sung:
how the rimshots of rain
& the bass line of wind

make more than a rhythm section
how the laughter of musicians
before the set is also a music
how the pretty girl suddenly
a beautiful woman makes
concentration tough all day

how the color green defies definition
is simply what it is
cannot be described
beyond the naming
beyond the singing
of green things

Teen Town

And now the band plays on
without its "fearless leader"

there is in the continuing
the need for change

change being the whole point
not staying put

not playing it safe
not a museum but a town of teens

who think they can't miss
and know they can

keeping it young
keeping it nervy

the band goes on

2.

The Branch Will Not Break, But the Jay Might

It's the first warm day of spring, my daughter
   was born two days ago, I'm looking down

from the second floor, and there's this jay
   shifting her balance in a small tree below me.

It reminds me of James Wright's jay, who knew
   the branch would not break.

Once we found a jay hanging upside down
   from a branch in the back yard.

You could spin him around and around.

Finally, my father knocked him down with a broom.

Hang on, my daughter, small and unbroken.

                3/28/85

The Economics of Small Losses

The toy car that turns into a robot
which was missing so long my son lost interest in it

turned up finally in the real car.
I like the symmetry of that, just like the wallet

we stopped looking for. It turned up in the down
quilt in the closet, but because of inflation

we found something different. Now the camera
is missing. It's not so much the camera,

it's the shots of the new baby—the small blue hands
have been lost. Tonight I can't find the cat.

I listen, lost in my listening, and think I hear him,
but it's the house still settling

or the fish tossing in its sleep.
If you repeat a word long enough it loses its meaning,

but you hear the sound better. There are compensations.
I hear the thump a cat makes jumping down,

but it's just the wind. Then, around the corner,
his green-gold eyes.

Midnight

for Peter

my son wakes up and
will not be comforted for
he believes the bad Volkswagen
will eat him
he believes the moonlit water tower
will take five giant steps
toward him
he believes the man with the white beard
will ask him a question

on the other hand
I believe the Volkswagen
which is neither good nor bad
will indifferently run me over
I believe the water tower will run dry
I believe the man with the white beard
will ask me a question
thus proving he knows everything
and I know nothing

in our stillness now
waiting for the house to ignite
this is our faith
this is our kinship

Home Movies

Some have come back from the grave
to do something as ordinary
as step off a porch.

Some have returned to claim
an innocence as bright and hard
as the snowballs malice could make.

And the maples toss easily here,
in this unfaithful light,
that now are unmoved by any storm.

Match Point

It's said Beckett
in his endgame

sat and watched tennis
on tv

singles
I assume and

the irony of zero
being called love

not lost on him
I'm sure

nor the rueful
possibility

of an eternal
deuce

Larkin

You knew
to take nothing
and make a poem of it
was to find something
worth the saying of it:

the real rage
of leaden days is seen
not in these pages
but the silence
you knew

between.

The Acting Program Director Holds a Press Conference to Explain the Death of the Challenger Shuttle and Seven Aboard in a Fiery Cloud of Snow

On the watch
beneath his starched cuff
numbers continue to change
matter is simply
energy at rest
a shift in infor-

mation just
as evidence of
shirtsleeve weather is brought to
our winter by a
systematic ar-
rangement of dots seen

from the right
distance his face fills
the plane of the screen while a
gull apparently
glides into his left
ear and out his right

Cold Harbor

seven thousand dead
in twenty minutes
a new American
outdoor record
even
for the Civil War
seven thousand cold
to the touch

some harbor

Poets in Their Youth

Everybody knew everybody.
When we went to the Cape,
the train sounded like Yeats.
Without trying, we all dressed in white.
After breakfast, we strolled to our sunlit rooms
and worked on our next coups until dinner.

Afterwards, we would have a conversation.
If Flaubert had been American,
where would he have gone to school?
(Brown, someone would finally chuckle.)
We measured our gin meticulously,
we smoked and married casually,

we rose and assumed our places, conversing
the whole comfortable length of the night,
and withdrew reluctantly, just before dawn,
to a privacy where we would plot,
in the last shades of darkness,
our legendary falls.

Blues

There was this: I saw,
beneath the gray monotony of sky
and high on the gray wall,
the huge crow that had uttered the cry
that made me look up;

and heard the answering call
of two raving toward him;
and heard, as he let go
and leapt up to join them,
the ragged wing scrape cement.

A.M.

although by now
convinced the world

is round there are
still moments not at

night but waking to
the drone of traffic

in the street
dumptrucks striving

through their gears
early birds out

for the quick kill
when I know

I could step right
off the edge and fall

Last Rites

we the living
tell the living

how young we
all look and we

the living
tell the living

how good the dead
look and the dead

say nothing

Four Poems About Distance, in Memory of My Father (1900-1989)

19N   026D

my father is sleeping

I move to the window   19 floors up
it's a landscape I know

but not from this distance

beyond the trees in the dark the water
and the lights on the water

headlights along the ribbon of road

building's steady exhaling

it's the zen of air travel   time
between coordinates of departure/arrival

automatic pilot

then I see in the glass
his face rising up

MY FATHER SLEEPING WAKING DRIFTING DYING

holds up
his wrist
where
his watch
would be
then
rubs his
flesh as
though
to see
whose time-
less
arm this
is that
swims
in the
empty
air

I AM AT A DISTANCE

driving in the long shadows of morning
not understanding the tormented expressions
of drivers who slip by next to me

but when I squint back toward the road
it's my father I happen to be following
his blue hardtop Dodge with the Triple A sticker

I see the lane is vague to him
he's drifting from side to side like someone tired
of trying to find the right word

I follow him past home
past the mall glittering in the early sun
through the waves of heat unfurling from farms

and onto the north road which is colder
orange and red maples flaring overhead his hand
is steady on the wheel now

both of us plunging into mad torrents of snow
the wiper blade groaning against the windshield
as the snow goes from falling to rising

he is jostled bouncing over the rutty white landscape
and I am beside him on the wide seat as we slow
and pull into the yard of the weathered gray house

well home again he announces as I run to greet him
his red hands fumble with the bicycle clips and brush
the packed snow from the folds of his pants

he takes my mother's hand and leads her into the dark
they emerge from the white country church shielding
their eyes from mad torrents of rice

I am at a distance and see my father against the sun
striding toward me his coat draped over his arm
emerging from the blinding glare waving almost singing

SOUTHERN PARKWAY

Driving east under a midnight promising snow,
    one week after your death,
we cruise comfortably between the pack of red taillights
                                              ahead
    and the mob of headlights behind.
It's a caution I chafed at as a son beside you in the dark,
    a safe distance that now I understand,
        having become the father of sons,
and take my gloves off (as you would) to better hold the
                                              wheel,
    and keep my eyes on home.

Untitled

Something is moving in the porch light—
fine rain or snow, I can't tell which.

Tonight you told me you've always rued
forgetting your mother's last wish—

that in those last hours the light be left on.
She wanted to watch the world to the end.

And it's easy to see, lost in grief
and astonishment, how in the hard leaving

it would be easy to walk past the nurse
and only absently nod, hearing the rain

driving in sheets against the windows.
That, like everything, can't be undone.

But that wasn't like everything.
It comes right up to the edge of words.

I've been starting books lately but can't go on,
going to readings and losing my place.

There are too many words, they're too easy.

"Say something funny, Ronald," she whispered to me.
And I, struck dumb, let her down too.

Lately

I hear the voice of
your mother who
always looked young
until suddenly old
with cancer talking to
my father who is
gone now too

where have they gone
our daughter asks

where

lately
we have become
the family who locks
the car with
the windows down

we have become
the family
of wasted tickets
empty seats

Song

It is exactly a year ago
day of my father's burial and
to not forget the not knowing
of so much that's all that matters
unembarrassed by art I listen to

Arvo Pärt's *Cantus in Memory of Benjamin Britten*
swept on the spiritstrings
on the cellosorrow and
can imagine a life lifting up
out of this one

Up From the Skies (as Hendrix would have it)
but the cat won't honor transcendence
won't leave me alone, rubbing, kneading,
wanting only the body's sweat
the living salt

       2/1/90

CVA

in memory of my mother

1. *ICU*

Walking back to the car,
the hospital lights are a beautiful constellation
rising up into the stars.

Here on earth,
in the red strobes of emergency,
your blank nods and swimming hand
make us murmur to each other:
She's doing better, there's some improvement....

Yesterday you even scrawled something
that looked like "very sick."

I try to imagine what you know and
I try to imagine what I know to be true
and what must be said.

There is a loud honesty that is in love
with itself that I'd like to avoid.

I've seen movies that have changed my life
and they're made of light,

brilliant lies shining in the dark.

2. *Night Visits*

I think that you are lost in dreams

I think that you have taken each part of your pain
    and found an image for it

and around that core stories spin like electrons
    like the wispy arms of galaxies

I think that this is where you live now
    beyond the air of mown lawns the sting of rain

        beyond our gravity

I think that you are in the dark now
    adrift somewhere between the fever of atoms

    and the singing of the stars

3.   *A Psalm*

Leaving the aluminum cold
of the hospital
the corruption

of the body and
into the noon light
a sparrow flits

from its bench slat
a quick improvisation
in air

the shadow across concrete
perfect in its
counterpoint

You leave us
with this praise:
the fact of sparrow

the fiction
of shadow and
what is between them

a harmony
which is the poem
the song

Coda: Self-Portrait With Cat and Hupmobile

There is a snapshot of me
squatting before the family car
with a childhood cat
which looks exactly like Roy
the cat we have now
forty years later

I consider time
the human sense of change
the cat poised
in its eternal now

thus the same boy
with a different cat
is also the same cat
with a different boy

but there are no more Hupmobiles

and you are not here

On the Death of Parents

I'm held by what survives—
a scribbled note saying "Be right back,"
glasses, teeth
grinning in a cup that cracked
but never broke—

obdurate facts, novelty items, sick jokes
piled up like junk mail
promising free installation,
hours of pleasure,
special rates.

Someone Stopped In

Someone else stopped in.
The boy put the books on the rug.
It will take an hour to set things right.

Yesterday the glasses snapped off,
soon a call must be made to the optician.
Today my son began to cry.

Someone called about subscribing.
There was soap to buy,
books to be stamped again at the library.

Someone stopped in and talked politics.
I bought a lightbulb with three positions.
And of course there is sex.

It's not much, I admit, but I'm going on.
Books explain the diminished seventh on C,
there is the continuation of the race to consider,

without good vision I will mistake shadows for owls.
There is the pleasure of a clean shirt,
the need at dusk for light.

3.

Blues in "C"

in memory: Gil Evans (1912-1988)

1.
It's the torque of a spring Sunday
wound against the eardrum, the first open window
letting outside in, late afternoon,
already the temperature beginning to dip,
the ferry heading out
sounding its pompous horn (though there is no fog,
just these late chords of light),
then answered
by the train rocking toward Port Jeff,
all the disparate sounds an uneasy harmony:
snarl of dirtbikes and power saws, motorcycles
showing off winding through their gears,
the yip of a mutt, swoosh of a convertible that leaves
in its wake dead leaves swirling among green buds,
and the blips of a video game take their place too,
as natural as the two crows outside the window
mocking in rough counterpoint,
or the voices
inside houses down the block, dim and pleading,
families reprising their sad histories....

2.

And I think of your late band, the dense variety
of sounds overlapping, stopping, starting, waiting,
the loose rhythms washing against one another,
moody and tidal,
nothing urgent to be resolved,
notes milling, out on a limb—
wisecracks, potshots, pratfalls—
then the wild facts gathered, shuffled, swung
into jet stream riffs above drum cauldrons
till precipitation! Hot rain of notes, sleet squalls,
then a shiver of alto joy down the spine of sorrow—
always up to the edge, whelming, striving,
then moving on,
a new timbre, shifting ground,
a lush dissonance bending toward a harmony,
as the sun goes, as *Blues in "C"* quiets finally,
like two friends tired of quarreling,
like the hush after testimony,
after desire...
Parabola life!

New song to the end!
The older you got, the younger it got.
The window thrust open,
song letting everything in...

3.
every day something happens
that's not supposed to happen
that's not on the calendar
not in the cards

it's the body breaking down
it's the boy in the well
too many ambulances in the bays
the window sealed by paint

sometimes I feel
like a mother of the pedestrian
no invention in sight
                  then the maya
of neon on rainy streets
the crackle of a flung shirt and
the electricity is back
                  even
the fictionist of sorrow
with the cult who adores his silence
begins to speak
                  the musician
who lays the horn down
to catch his breath
and waits five years
picks it up and sings
                  a blues
so ardent the notes so true
they make you smile
(in a parenthesis of pain)
the smile of consent

4.
The whisper of sprinklers has stopped,
water eddies along the curb, it's laced with soap bubbles
(the humming carwashers have gone inside)
in whose sheen
are reflected the white clouds
and the blue heavens imperceptibly turning darker,
darker: and it is quiet now.

And it is quieter now.